WOMAN'S WORK
Poems, Songs, and Hope for the Journey

Marie Chewe-Elliott

Woman's Work: Poems, Songs & Hope for the Journey

• • •

Marie Chewe-Elliott

Copyright © 2016 Marie Chewe-Elliott
All rights reserved.

ISBN: 1533667020
ISBN 13: 9781533667021

Woman's Work: Becoming our best selves

• • •

I chose the title "Woman's Work," because I recall how my paternal grandfather would designate certain domestic tasks --cooking, cleaning, childcare, etc.,-- as "woman's work." He would say it, as if those vital tasks were too lowly for men but should be priority for women. Without a doubt, our families and homes are priority but, I also expect this to be a priority for my spouse.

My grandfather was born in 1911, in an age of different expectations, social mores and standards based on gender, so I am inclined to forgive him – mostly. He saw being home as a priority for women because he believed it ultimately was the only acceptable option. It is no secret that some version of this double standard exists today, even though nearly 60 percent of American women over 16 are in the workplace. This means that many of us are working 50 hours a week for our employers and about the same when we get home. We have bought into the myth of superwoman and it is killing us. We work on or work out everything for everyone else, except ourselves. We are missing the opportunity to create our greatest masterpiece when we neglect working on making ourselves whole.

In 2016, we are stressed, overworked, overwhelmed, burned out and burning the proverbial candle at both ends. Because we have accepted the unrealistic standards that taught us to be all things to all people, ALL THE TIME, we prioritize everything and everyone else above ourselves. We have done this at the peril of our own physical, emotional, financial and sometimes even spiritual well-being. We are masters at working miracles for our families and employers, when we really should be working on ourselves. One of our greatest challenges is to take time and make time to do our own work.

What kind of work, you ask? That answer is different for each of us and we have the responsibility to understand what work we must do to become the best version of ourselves that's possible. Part of my "work" is giving voice to women and the things that celebrate us, concern us, uplift us – HEAL us. My "work" also includes being mindful of those behaviors, practices and rituals that nurture me and nourish my spirit. That can mean taking time for massage, meditation or a writing workshop. It can also mean confronting, owning and addressing my own shortcomings with courage and resolving to do better. It can mean learning to say, "no," BEFORE I'm overwhelmed.

What does your work look like? Insecurity? Face it and address it. Health issues or unresolved family issues? Face it and address it. Deal with it TODAY. I pray that you'll be able to answer and embrace your journey. Like the instructions we receive before a flight to put the oxygen mask on ourselves FIRST, we must be our own priority and save ourselves before we can help all those who depend on us.

We are worth the work.

• • •

Thanks and Acknowledgements

• • •

SPECIAL THANKS TO MY FAMILY for reading or listening to each poem and not reminding me of how many times you've previously listened to them. You already know I wouldn't attempt to do any of this without your help and support. Mike, Mikki. Maris, Pat, Mom & Dad, Kim, Kenosha for everything you had to do for me or with me because I was trying to write. You know I can't help myself.

Editor, Tonya Smith: Thank you for your work and attention to detail and making my poems better. Forgive me for putting your English degree to work.

Stephanie Garrison Polston: What can I say about the cover? You made me cry with your visual interpretation of my work. I am so grateful for the role you played in completing, "Woman's Work."

Charlotte Beard at Get It in Writing, LLC: I appreciate your work and look forward to working with you again.

Thank you to every reader for your continued support of my work. I appreciate each email, note or invitation to speaking or reading events. You keep me motivated and encouraged to keep doing this. Let me know if something strikes a chord with you or touches your heart. You can email me at myelliott61@gmail.

• • •

Table of Contents

Woman's Work: Becoming our best selves	v
Thanks and Acknowledgements	vii
Granny's Sankofet	1
Empress *(Tribute to Katherine Dunham)*	2
Algoma	3
Wedding March	4
After Katrina	6
Wall of Remembrance	7
Untitled	8
Morning Prayer	9
Yes, Jesus Loves Me	11
Juneteenth	14
Song for Sistahs	17
Season	19
Xtreme Love Poem (You) *written with Kim Moore*	20
2014	22
Headlines 2008	24
Mississippi	27
Up Above My Head	29
Love Note	31
Love Note #2	32
Love Note #3	33
Black **Bra**	34
Season's Greetings	35
Final Destination	36
Metamorphosis of Vanessa Cardui (Painted Lady Butterfly)	37
Hearts Dance Home	38

Women Warriors	39
Locks n' Life	40
Moving	41
Prayer of the Saints	42
Rain on Me	44
New Mercies	45
Girlfriends	46
More Than Enough	49
About the author	51

Granny's Sankofet

Hands like tanned leather
Reincarnate to command
Mezzo forte renditions of Baptist standard hymns
From days gone by
What a Friend We Have in Jesus and Glory to His Name
Granny's voice refuses silence and
Speaks long after she is gone

Gone to heavenly reward for reading and living according to the Word
Drilled aspiring doctors, teachers, writers, with speeches
for Easter, Christmas and Children's Day programs
From days gone by
Breathed life into gooey Algoma mud planted love reared children
Harvested sorghum, melons, tomatoes and corn
Stitched patchwork couture and the foundation of generations

Generations will cherish and channel her spirit
Great-greats will sing the songs and prayers of her lips,
Beckon the values and blessings
From days gone by
Arms spread wide gather
Then cradle the bountiful
Legacy from her heart to our hands

Empress *(Tribute to Katherine Dunham)*

All hail
the Empress with skin hued like honey
alluring eyes
platinum crowning glory
feet agile as hands
transformed to hallow
any place her sole/soul landed.

Haiti to East Saint…
"5-6-7-8" Ibo, Mahi, plies
Come hither movement of
Congo Paillette,
double-step, triplets.

All hail
rhythmic cadence sounds,
palm leaves strewn on red carpet
blanket the ground
American Beauty roses rain down
bodies rock and roll
legs circle and swing
The Empress has entered
The new Jerusalem.

Algoma

Above the white noise of
Salvation Army bell ringers
And Christmas songs about
Santa and reindeer
The call of drums wake me
To remembrance of
royal former selves and
rebirth of dreams forgotten.

Voices in dialects unknown,
Yet familiar, beckon
And I follow
pathways to the Nguzo Saba.

Villagers spread loving arms to
Children with no one to embrace.
Hands and hearts
Extend to elders with
dimming vision and
abbreviated footsteps.

Weathered hands grasp for me
Through gooey white Algoma mud
and the ages.
I kiss them, then bow in reverence.
Like metal to magnet
I am drawn to drink the libation of knowledge
Praying to see
The ancestors again
In me.

Wedding March

Tsunami
War
Global warming
Darfur
Yet we believe in love.

Life shifts like
Faults at
Epicenter of New Madrid
yet the sunshine of
your love blinds me.

Vera Wang dress
2 karats set in platinum
Enhance our bliss
But are not essential
To the work of the
Master Craftsman.

It is He who
Orchestrated me to you
You to me
Assigned our meeting
Merging, mating
Dissolved us from
Two to one.

Standing before friends
And kin
We submit and commit
Walk the aisle
Jump the broom
Into His everlasting love.

After Katrina

Seven days after Katrina
We were moonstruck.

From St. Louis and Pittsburgh
We panned the horizon
And discovered a dim crescent sliver
Pasted to infinite black canvas.

"It's so beautiful, it doesn't even look real,"
Kenosha said.
She was excited like she'd found an old friend.
I, too, was comforted by the sight.
Like a drifting fisherman
Spotting a beacon's light.

Perhaps the familiar
Means our world
Will be all right.

Wall of Remembrance

I.

Trayshaun Harris*Travante Greely*Joshua Harris*Precious Doe aka Erica Michelle Marie Green* Gina Dawn Brooks* Conner Peterson* Matthew Shepherd* Rilya Wilson * Jon Benet Ramsey* Christian Ferguson * Zariah Unique Harrison* Michael and Alex Smith * Noah, John, Paul, Luke and Mary Yates* Chandra Levy* Jessica Lunsford* Dominic Williams* Heather Kullorn* Dylan Groen*Daphne Philisia Jones* Natalee Holloway* Rilya Wilson* Isiah Barber* Braydon Barnes*Jamyla Bolden

II.

No chatter, clatter
Pitter-patter
No pageant crowns
Silenced giggles and
Muzzled baby sounds
No prom dates
Coming in late
No Barbies or Bratz
Tonka ® trucks
Graduation caps
Animal crackers
Flashing clackers
Missing
Eclipsed youngsters
Snuffed out
Like candlelight.

Untitled

I am a single starfish
Riding waves in the Atlantic,
A lone petal in the Rose Parade,
A solitary ant at the July 4th picnic
Daring to believe
In my significance
Naïve enough to
Believe that you love me.

Morning Prayer

It's 5 a.m. when I rise,
Shake off sleep,
Pry open my eyes.
Marvel at the sun, the clouds,
The skies.

Behold the blessing of a new day
Then chastise the cat
Warn the kid about being late
And get on my way.

Flip to CNN
Share java with the hubby, then
Stop to hear a Robin sing
Or was it my angel
Just doing her thing?

Angel…Oh God forgive me
I didn't pray
So let me start by saying
Thanks for your amazing grace.
For keeping the family all night long,
forgiving me when I think and act wrong
Covering me when my resistance isn't strong.
I surely need you with me
As I do all that's ahead
Be my strength
Anoint my hands, my feet,
Every thought that comes in my head.

Marie Chewe-Elliott

Help me be what you want me to be.
More things to thank you for
Than I can even name
And blessings keep raining
Down on me.
So I praise and lift you up
Your love overflows my cup.
Keep me in your care
Stay with me everywhere.
In Jesus name I pray.
Amen!

Yes, Jesus Loves Me

*"Yes Jesus loves me, Yes Jesus loves me,
Yes Jesus loves me, For the Bible tells me so."*

From an early age most of us are consumed with the idea of love. One of the first notes youngsters pass each other in school queries, "Do you love me? Yes or no. Check the box." Many of us spend a lifetime asking or wondering that same question. Writers of hundreds of secular songs have stirred us with love songs like, "Endless Love, Mighty Love, Lovin' You" I believe the answer lies in the first little song we learned as children…

We are heiresses to the love in John 3:16
A love never before seen
And it's an awesome and magnificent thing.
True love that lets me call
Without His cell, email or URL.

You know true love that makes me
Show kindness and patience to enemies and friends
And assures me that He's with me until the end.
So whether friendship and romance fades
This divine and immeasurable love remains the same.

Love that let's me not worry about speaking in tongues
But about speaking a word or peace
To a that hurting brother or sister
Whether in our sanctuary or in the street.

Marie Chewe-Elliott

True love like when Jesus purposely
Waited on the woman at the well
The gave her a secret
She had to tell.

True love that blinds me
To others' faults
And makes me keep silent
When I ought.

Love makes me cry
When I think of him dying on the cross
Snatching me out of sin
So my soul
Wouldn't be lost

Love that nudged us awake
Kept the hubby and babies safe
Love that makes wild flowers bloom
With no fertilizer or pruning.
Love so compelling that I don't want to go
Into with ease
But I want to FALL head over heels
Follow
Anywhere
Lord
Leads.

Love that makes me forgive more
Makes me release a grudge
Love that makes me look in mirror and see
It took His love to come from above

Wrapped in love as a baby
Then go to Calvary
To save a sinner like me.

In the words of the song writer
"When nothing else could help
Love lifted me."
Not only lifted me
But cleaned me up, then set me free.

Today as a grown woman, I recall
The words taught to me long ago
"Yes, Jesus loves me, for the Bible
tells me so."

Juneteenth

Part I (young Mary)
Celebrate! Celebrate! Word is come of
The order to emancipate.

Don't hesitate, it's time to Celebrate!
This order called the
Emancipation Proclamation
Frees people of color all over the nation.

Emancipate? Why, it means freedom.
Freedom done finally come for us—
I knew it would because it was in
The good Lawd that we put our trust.

I heard tell that word came down from
Massa Lincoln himself
By General Gordon Granger who said:
*Under the Honorable President Lincoln and
The power vested in me I
declare that all slaves are free
effective January 1863.*

II (Aunt Nannie)

'cuse me. Did you say 1863?
Child it's 1865.
So you're telling me
That the last two years

Of my heartache and tears
Didn't have to be
I was free, back in 1863?

Free to read, write,
Make my own rules
Take my 40 acres and my mule.

Don't know where I'se goin'
But I'se sho' leavin here
Get my song and shout on
Celebrate and cheer.

Gonna sang when the spirit
Say sang and learn to read Gawd's Word
No more hidin my Holy Book under the wash tub.
Gonna farm my own land
Stand up for myself and be treated
Like a woman—

And I'se still a woman
Despite 40 years of working like a dog
Takin' care of Massa's crops,
tending the cows, sloppin the hogs…
seein' my chillun sold
All for naught.

Slavery was evil and jes plain wrong!!
Didn't know I'd live to see the day
When I'd fling my arms high as heaven
Wide as the sea
Sing my hallelujahs

Marie Chewe-Elliott

And say, "We's Free! We's Free!
Glory to Gawd
We's Free!

Song for Sistahs

Here's a song for Sistahs
Waiting for the bus, and
Waving hi and bye to the rest of us
As we Jag by, Benz away or put our
Trust in Lexus.

So I sing for the Sistah raising child number three
Without the babies' daddy
While getting' her G.E.D
But dreamin of her Ph.D.

Sing for Sistahs
Like my Granny and Big Mama who fought and scratched
Their way out of segregation and miseducation,
Race and sex discrimination
With nothing but a good old-fashioned
Hymn, scripture and determination
Like *What a Friend We Have in Jesus*…you know the rest.
GOD SO LOVED THE WORLD HE GAVE HIS ONLY BEGOTTEN SON…
Greater is He that is in me, than he that is in the world.

Sing for the Sistahs who are traumatized and criticized every day of life.
SOMEone, SOMEwhere always finds SOMEthing wrong with us.
We're too black, too fat, Talk too loud or too white/right.

Sing and pray for the Sistah whose
Life is helter skelter
Or broke down to her last dime
Now living in the shelter.

Marie Chewe-Elliott

Sing for the crack-head, prostitute, battered or displaced Sistah,
Sing like she's your mother, friend or soror.
Sing because at least you're happy
Sing because you're free
Sing because that sistah, my sistah
Could be you or me!

Season

Monday changed to Friday.
Summer to fall.
All day, I wait
For your call.

Leaves waltz and twirl
outside my window.
Flaunting coats of gold,
sienna and crimson.

I wonder if your love
has changed
like the season.

Xtreme Love Poem (You)
written with Kim Moore

Sunsets, you
Dreamscapes, you
I sleep
Then wake with you
On my mind.
Drive 75 in the rain
In the 55 lane
With you
On my mind.

Alarms sounds, you
Work, you
I call in sick
Cause my heart hurts
From beating for you so hard.
I race to the phone
When I hear your ringtone.

Play, you.
Then hang on the phone
all night
Silently
Because you want me to.

Breathe you,
Can't imagine without you.
My heart, you.
See, I fell for you
Into zero gravity and
My feet haven't touched
The ground since your
Lips touched mine.

I love you like Usain loves track
Like midnight loves black
Like King Kong loves
The blond woman
Like flowers love sun
And I won't deny it
I'm not ashamed
Cause you promised me a ring
And your last name.
I love you like Christ
Loves the church
From Alpha to Omega and
Unconditionally.
And I ain't going no where
Until my heart says the same.

2014

I've been here before
Down through the ages
To this place, this stage
On the threshold of justice's door

Praying, marching, shouting
Knock, knock, knocking
Waiting and wading knee-deep then waist-high
through the tears of the mothers
knowing there will be others.
Praying, marching, shouting.
Yes, I have been here before
On the threshold of justice's door
Half a century ago
In Selma, Oxford
And Birmingham.
Choking down indescribable rage
I gasp for air then
Dial 9-1-1 to resuscitate justice in New York, Sanford, Ferguson.
The call is unanswered and I know
The tears of the mothers will not bring them back
Marching, shouting, praying will not bring them back
There is no protection for driving while black, walking while black
or just BE-ING black in America.
I can't breathe knowing there will
Be others.
Like Schwerner, Chaney and Goodman
Emmett, Medgar, Martin,
Like Trayvon, Michael and Eric

Who became casualties of war
On liberty and justice for some.
I have been here before
And the young ones say
We must dropkick the door.
Hands up and
And hearts aflame
hold on to justice
Like Nimbostratus
clouds hold rain.

Declaring never to visit
This place again.

Headlines 2008

Reading the day's headlines
Makes me sad—
Then mad as:

Body bags
Caskets draped with flags bring 1000
Soldiers back to tiny, one-horse sites
For interment and last rites;

Galleries of b-roll and
Still photos
document the horror of
Declaring unnecessary war
With no allies
On our side;

Hungry children in our town.
And food is parachuted
To the ground
In Afghanistan;

45 million Americans
without healthcare funds
$230 billion to
invade, rebuild Iraq and
find Saddam;

Mothers, fathers, sons and daughters
Put their safety in question
For weapons of mass destruction
Not yet found.

And in today's news…
Illiteracy and neglect pervade crumbling schools
But prayer and discipline do not.
Homeless mothers deliver uncelebrated
babies into trash cans or toilets;

Luxury autos come standard with GPS
Yet there is no system for tracking
Young Christian Ferguson
Who has vanished without a trace.

Jobs are outsourced or relocated
To Bangladesh, Taiwan
All in name of free trade.
Alan Keys hops
On the GOP auction block
In a desperate effort to
Beat Barack

Courts and conservative campaigns
Attempt to make my sexual orientation and
position on abortion
Matters of political consideration or
Religious affiliation.

Marie Chewe-Elliott

Homeless mothers
Deliver unheralded babies
into the trash
Illiteracy and neglect
crumble our schools

And I'd be a fool
To subject myself to
Four more years of this.

So I read the headlines
Become sad…I also get mad.
Mad enough to vote
And ask myself
"Am I better off now,
than 4 years ago?"
I make a mental note
And say, "Hell no!"

Stench of pregnant chads
Untallied votes and a president-*select*
Wraps this election
Like a baby's blanket.

Reading the headlines makes me sad
Then mad enough to remember
That folks died for my right to vote
If I stay home and
get four more years of the same
I have only myself to blame.
Because as hailed
By a recent mass email
"No one died
When Clinton lied."

Mississippi

Home is where indigo skies are untouched by pollution and kudzu and fireflies decorate an already picturesque landscape.

Cotton bolls stand tall like atop stalks sprouting up out of rich, fertile earth and folks use yestidy, over yonder and y'all with no consideration for grammarians rules;
Where traces of the Confederacy still speak loudly. And historic antebellum mansions with lily white columns tower majestically above magnolia blossoms and acres of soybean—much like masters of old must have hovered over my laboring ancestors in these same fields.

Here houses are located on narrow streets and sometimes even on a gravel road; and everybody knows all the residents in their town, knows their names, all their business and how long the family has been around;

Where Blacks survived Bilbo and Barnette
where marches, sit-ins and
fighting for civil rights,
resulted in Medgar's death.

And despite racists threats and predictions
We lived to tell of James Meredith's and Ole Miss' integration.
Where news of Emmett Till's brutal death
and that of three civil rights workers shocked an entire nation.

Home is where Fannie Lou Hamer got tired of being sick and tired and decided to vote.
It is here that family members who migrated north or west in the 50s and 60s return each year for family reunions and exploring their roots.

Home is the Baptist church where I was saved, baptized and wed.
Where treetops once reeked with the stench of lychings, hangings and bloodshed; the source of Morris' **Yazoo** and Moody's **Coming of Age.**
It is the place I think of on scorching July days,
The aroma at Big Mama's house of collard greens, cornbread and caramel cakes;
Where friends and I invaded clubs and partied every Saturday night,
Then roles early for Sunday morning worship to try and get our souls back right.

Here I matured and learned of love, hate, racism and pain
Family, friends, church picnics, and farmers and gardeners praying for rain.

It is here my mind wanders in the cool of the day
Back to Mississippi,
Even though I'm far away.

Up Above My Head

Up above my head
I hear poetry in the air.
Up above my head
I hear poetry everywhere.

In reggae and pop
Even rap, gospel and hip-hop
Everywhere I look
Poetry gets me with the "hook,"
Like "the revolution will not be televised."
How do I love thee, let me count
The ways or… Floetry's
All you gotta do is say yes.

Be it the skee doo dee ah of jazz
The soulfulness of neosoul or
The lonliness of (strum) the blues.

Poetry struts in like an arrogant lover,
Barely acknowledges my presence
Then messes with my mind
Locks a rhythm makes me
Leave my inhibitions behind.

It comes closer
Massages my temples
Caresses my hand
Then leads me (consentingly)
To poetry land.

Marie Chewe-Elliott

Up above my head
I see poetry in the air
Up above my head
Poetry traipses the globe and
Follows me everywhere.
I see it in a dance when
No music is playing,
Makes me splish, splash in a puddle
During a rain
In the clap and boom of God's
Thunder and lightning –
Even though it's frightening.
In my little cousin's infectious giggle
Or that ticklish way a lady bug wiggles
On my finger.
Poetry always speaks to me
Serenades me
With sonnets, haiku,
Ballad, soliloquy.

The *me—ow* of Twinkle, our cat
The queenly way the church mothers
Parade their hats.

Perhaps I'm being stalked
Poetry seems to be everywhere!
Even in the mall! On a cloud, on a star

Inhale, now exhale slowly.
Can you smell it, hear it, taste it?
Poetry is in the air.
Surely, there's a poetry God somewhere!

Love Note

Clarity comes
When I rest
On your chest or
Snuggle in the cusp of your arms.

Chaos reemerges
And reality sets in.
I must go
Or you must go
And my heart breaks.

Part here,
Part with you.
One foot in, one foot out.
I oscillate between
the lives that separate us
And the one we ponder.

Love Note #2

Can't look into your eyes and
Quench my desire
To lie in your arms
Submit to your charm

Can't hold your hand in mine
Without thirsting for your lips
Just one more time

Your fragrance makes me giddy
Your baritone melts
My weak resistance and
I'm not ashamed to say
I never regretted loving you
Not even for a day.

Love Note #3

With gentle kisses
I bandage your heartbreak and
Bathe you in comfort.

Hand in hand I touch
The crevices of your spirit
And together we soar

I taste your pain
Extract the same
Nourish you to
love again

Black Bra

Like a true friend
You're with me to the end
Embracing all of me
Making me love the skin
I'm in.

I sure do love you
Always thinking of you.
Wrapped in your care
I go everywhere.

Wearing yellow, pink or white
You make it alright.

With you I feel
Like a million bucks
You put the diva bounce
In my strut.

Soma, Cacique, Curvations
You enhance my curves
Lift my … situation.

You know I love
Always thinking of you.
Black bra, black bra.

Season's Greetings

Airbrushed snowflakes form
geometric designs across the sky.
The fire crackles and dances as
Youngsters delight hearing of
Cupid, Rudolph and Prancer.
Though promotions are unremitting
for toys, gems and other material things
the season is about the birth of Jesus
And the joy He brings.

Final Destination

How shall we meet Jesus in the air?
Will we turn noses upward and
Ascend like we're aboard Delta, Northwest or ComAir?

Will we go up, up, up
Til we hear Jesus say,
"Good evening ladies and gentleman
I've made the sun shine today
And for the next two hours we'll be cruising at 26,000 feet.
I'm gonna take you higher higher higher than ever before.
We're going to cruise right on up to heaven's door!"
I wonder if, as I step past the clouds
I will even bother to look down.
Will I say "From this altitude the cars all look like ants?"

Will I look at the maze
of streets and rivers and be reminded of
The tedious journey I've made?

As I go up, up and away
On the judgment day
I will look back,
look up and be grateful that when
I was in the depths of sin
God snatched me in the nick of time,
auto-piloted my life and changed my mind.

Metamorphosis of Vanessa Cardui (Painted Lady Butterfly)

If you met me before my rebirth then
Perhaps you will not recognize the Painted Lady Butterfly I have become.
The span and strength of my wings will amaze you
as I ably soar just out of your grasp
and that of anyone who would hold me down or back..
My beauty might hypnotize you,
my ability to touch the heart of everyone who glimpses me
may cause you envy.
You may attempt to cast me aside again
as I did the cocoon
Which sheltered and protected me from
Rains and storm or any trauma that would cause me harm.
Just as life and the anticipation of blossoming on my own
Became too large for the cocoon,
So has my love for self
Eclipsed the darkness brought by you.

Hearts Dance Home

Hearts dance home in
Two-step. cha cha slide or
Harlem shake

Hearts dance home to hugs,
Babies' giggles and babble.
Hearts dance home to Mama's dressing,
Greens with smoked turkey and Graceland.

Hearts dance home to love
Hearts dance home to
Parties, birth of babies,
50th anniversaries, graduations
family situations.

Hearts dance home to love,
Cousins, sibling rivalries, forgiveness
Hearts dance home to love
Hearts dance home to
Hearts dance home.

Women Warriors

Women warriors watch
Fiercely over babies and home.

Women warriors watch and pray
As others move blindly.

Women warriors nurture,
Feed, embrace the unlovable.

Women warriors are fearless
Women warriors are swift
Women warriors rock.
Beware!
Women warriors
Will not be stopped!

Locks n' Life

I'm NOT Goldilocks!
In fact, my locs sometimes parallel my life.

Things are all relaxed and smooth
Then a rainstorm comes.
My stuff goes flat, then kinks up and blows up
Like an afro. A BIG, BEAUTIFUL, Angela Davis, 70s afro

Being the queen that I am, though,
I put Royal Crown on my locs,
Crown Royal in my cup
And relax again.

With head held high,
I open my mouth, taste the rain
then strut down the street
defying the storm.

Moving

Tacked wooden crates,
Bulging boxes
Sealed with Scotch tape

Conceal inside
Fragments of my worldly possessions
brass, crystal, porcelain
fragments of my life
faded photographs, college degrees
sentiments and love letters
from days gone by.

No décor left on the walls,
linen folded, draperies packed
nothing left at all

Empty ---
Like me inside
Each time

I relocate.

Prayer of the Saints

This evening our Heavenly Father,
here am I, your meek and humble servant
who is knee-bound and body-bent one more time.

Lord, I'm not before you because I've been so holy,
neither because I kept your commandments so well
but Fa------------------ther, I just want to say, "thank you."

Thank you for dispatching your angels
to camp around my bedside all night long.
Thank you because the bed I slept in
Was not my cooling board.
Thank you for letting me rise today
and start another day's journey --- Lord, I'm glad about it!
You even gave me a portion of health and strength and thennnnnnn----------------
I looked around and found that my family circle was yet unbroken and I had a bit of food on the table.

I realize it was your grace and mercy that kept me
from my earliest existence up to this present time.
I ask a special prayer for my husband and children.
Please be a fence of protection around them every day.
Go with them and stand by them every step of the way.
Anddddddddd___keep them out of the hands of wicked and unreasonable men.
Lord, I also ask you to bless my neighbors and my neighbors' children.

Please visit the sick and afflicted all over the land.
Go inside the prison walls and stir somebody's heart to say,
What must I do to be saved?"
Let them know that you are a heart-fixer and a mind regulator.
Let them know you are a_____ble to be
whatever they need you to be.
Able to be a mother to the motherless,
father to the fatherless,
a friend to the friendless.

In the words of the old song, Lord, I'm asking you
God, to please bless America. Our families are in turmoil, our schools are without a prayer and our world, as we know it, is at war. But God, your power supersedes the Commander-in-Chief, and the Defense Secretary because you are the King of Kings.

Now, Lord, when I've stacked up my hymnbooks and Bibles for the last time, I ask your grace on me – the least of all your servants and chiefest of all sinners.

Please grant me a peaceful hour in your kingdom, where I'll forever give you the praise. These and other blessings I ask in the matchless name of Jesus.

AMEN!

Rain on Me

Rain pummels my window pane, drenches the foliage and landscape décor.
Drip, drop, dripping on walkers, joggers and tourists
meandering down St. Charles Street.

Falls down on me
like the Holy Spirit saturated my soul at the Superdome
as my thirst was quenched for love, direction and protection.
Challenged me to be thinking,
challenged me to be delivered
from manipulation and tribulation.

Challenged me never to be the same after
Running to the water to be baptized,
Not to care if I am criticized
For seeking HIM.

Feel like I'm walking on air
or the wings of a prayer
Can hardly hold my peace because
my cup is yet overflowing.

New Mercies

Dawn evolves from black, pink, gray.
I pour my java, flip open the blinds, in awe of
God's unveiling of another day.

Skeletal silhouettes of oak, maple and pine
prop against the landscape as the rain
brushes teardrop designs on my windowpane.

Is my amazement His way
of reminding me of the new mercies
Covering me today?

Girlfriends

Through the friendship of women
I learned to socialize, fellowship,
Be criticized and analyze relationships.

Hide-and-seek
Simon Says or Trick-or-Treat
Slumber parties, slam books
Getting on each other's nerves
Exchanging dirty looks – it wouldn't have
Been the same without girlfriends.

Piano lessons and recitals, basketball and band
Learning to type and even shorthand.
Styling hair, polishing nail
Sharing our secrets and dreams
Mapping out our futures,
Picking our first pierced earrings.
Learning the Girl Scout promise,
Playing paper dolls
Telling after the first kiss
Modeling our dresses for prom.

Visiting colleges and praying
To get in
It was all better
With girlfriends.

Having babies that look
Just like us
Wondering how the man we love so much
Can sometimes make us want to curse.

Surviving love, learning to pay the rent
Meeting at the gravesites of relatives
And grandparents.

No matter what transcends
It's all easier with girlfriends.

More Than Enough

• • •

MY PRECIOUS SISTERS:

Embrace this phase of your life and know that you –just as you are today – are enough. "Enough?" you may ask. Yes, enough! You are smart **enough**, good **enough**, beautiful **enough** to become your best version of you and all you are meant to be. It is important that you find a way of conveying and reaffirming this message to yourself every day.

If you can do this, you will be well-equipped for those days when you FEEL you can't bear your heartbreak, make anyone happy or do anything right. Challenging days will surely come and like David at Ziklag, (*1 Samuel 30:6*) you must be prepared to encourage yourself. In the midst of your confusion, complication or crisis, you will have to get up, stand up and speak a word over yourself. And you must do this, especially when you feel you *cannot* do it. It will take a little practice and you may want to rephrase or repackage my words, but I encourage you to take a few seconds each day to look in the mirror and just declare to yourself that you are enough.

Start by identifying any area, characteristic or circumstance that has ever made you feel inadequate. What is it? Family issues, body image and self-esteem, your neighborhood? It doesn't matter!!! Fill in the blank and practice now:

"I am _____ enough and I will make it." Now say it until you believe it because it is true. (*Romans 8:28-30 and Philippians 4:13*). Repeat this again the next day and the next.

If you master this or some version of this you will be prepared when negativity or crises arise and dare attack your very existence.

Once you are comfortable with the fact that you are enough, you will be ushered into the amazing revelation that not only are you enough but you are MORE than enough. You are the cup overflowing, a gushing, drenching waterfall, the manifested hopes and prayers of mothers, grandmothers and aunties, the bridge to the future.

You – just as you are today – are who we once were
You – are God's vision
And you are MORE THAN ENOUGH!!

● ● ●

About the author

• • •

MARIE CHEWE-ELLIOTT IS A WRITER and poet in St. Louis, MO. She is the author of **Psalms of a Woman: Selected Poems & Reflections** and a children's book, **What Kittens Like**.

She is a graduate of the University of Mississippi and Webster University.

• • •

About the illustrator:
Stephanie Polston is an artist and art educator from St. Louis, MO. Her cover art was inspired by the book's rhythmic and colorful reminders to celebrate life, love and faith, even through moments of uncertainty.

• • •